Spicy
Salsas & Moles

Published by Familius LLC, www.familius.com
PO Box 1249, Reedley, CA 93654

Familius books are available at special discounts for bulk purchases, whether for sales promotions or for family or corporate use. For more information, contact Familius Sales at orders@familius.com.

Library of Congress Control Number: 2024936184

Print ISBN 9781641708920
EPUB ISBN 9798893960211

Printed in China

Edited by Peg Sandkam and Abby W. Tree
Cover design by Brooke Jorden
Book design by Brooke Jorden and Maggie Wickes

10 9 8 7 6 5 4 3 2 1

First Edition

Spicy Salsas & Moles

A COOKBOOK FOR LOVERS OF MEXICAN HEAT

ERICKA SANCHEZ & NICOLE PRESLEY

To my husband Efrain.
You are the salsa to my tacos.
Thank you so much for adding so much spice to my life.
—*Ericka*

To my entire *familia*,
may our family forever continue to pass our
traditions down and keep growing closer.
—*Nicole*

Contents

INTRODUCTIONS

I received my first molcajete on my wedding day. It was my grandmother's before she passed away. My mother traveled from Mexico to California carrying fifteen pounds of lava rock. It sat unwrapped on the gift table, worn, waiting to be taken home and serve its purpose—to make flavorful, spicy salsas with lots of love and devotion.

But the truth is, it made its way to the back corner of my apartment's kitchen.—in a dark and dusty cabinet. For years I opened and closed that cabinet. The molcajete peeked behind beer mugs and old coffee cups. I was intimidated. Although my grandmother wasn't here anymore, I was afraid to disappoint her. My salsas would never be as good as hers.

When my son was born, that molcajete was promoted to fruit bowl. The colorful bananas and mandarins masked my fear and intimidation for a couple of years. Although molcajete wasn't serving its purpose, it was still being displayed and utilized in a beautiful way—even if it was just a fruit bowl.

One day, I felt a tug. Something drew me to the molcajete. I purchased a root brush and cleaned every pebble and dried chile seed from its deep, dark crevices. I called my mom, and she walked me through every step and technique she learned from my grandmother on how to make salsa.

I practiced for years. With every attempt, I grew more confident, and my salsas tasted better and better. So here we are today. My grandmother would be proud of how far I've come and how her molcajete was my inspiration for this book.

Many of the traditional recipes in this book are my grandmother's and my mother's—the spicy ones in particular! But I created my own too, many with fruit and readily available ingredients. Salsa should be effortless but at the same time complex with different levels of flavor and heat. From burning hot, to smoky, to sweet, to tart. There is something for everyone.

I hope you enjoy this book as much as I loved being inspired from it. All you must do is start!

Happy salsa making!

—Erieka

Long live the flavor of chile that us Latinos cannot get enough of! From salsa to enchilada sauce, these are the recipes that represent my upbringing. Long after my great-grandparents crossed the Mexican border to the United States in search of a more stable life, my family continues to pass on our traditions. Keeping tradition alive was a big deal for my grandfather, who kept our family rooted in our Mexican heritage through food and the Spanish language (some of us speak it more fluently than others). As Mexican Americans living in Los Angeles, we have always struggled with living a dual culture. I was never Mexican enough (especially with the last name Presley) for people born in Mexico, and I was never American enough for the general market here in the United States.

The truth is, I am one-hundred percent proud to be a Chicana born in East Los Angeles who is very American and Mexican at the same time. I am proud of the Latinos living stateside who keep the Mexican food culture and heritage alive on this side of the border with the resources and ingredients available to us. If it wasn't for the Chicano population making Mexican food a mainstay in the United States, I don't think those food traditions would be as prominent as they are today, and that's something I don't think we are given enough credit for.

This brings us back to salsas and other Mexican food. I live to keep these spicy recipes alive and hope this publication will continue to be passed down from my generation to many that are still to come because Mexican spice should be celebrated on both sides of the border. If you don't have a molcajete, just make the salsa in the blender . . . it's the flavor that matters in the end.

—

HOW–TO PREP AND SEASON A NEW MOLCAJETE

Before using a new molcajete, it is necessary to "cure" or remove all excess rock material. This will prevent food that is prepared in it from being contaminated.

—Ericka

Step 1: Soak the molcajete in water for 2 hours.

Step 2: Scrub the molcajete with a brush and a pea-size amount of dishwashing soap. Rinse and set out to dry completely in the sun.

Step 3: Place 1/4 cup rice in the molcajete and crush into smaller pieces, grinding the surface of the molcajete in a circular motion. Repeat this step until the rice grinds clean with no visible traces of molcajete dust or gravel. Rinse with warm water.

Step 4: To season the molcajete, place 6 peeled cloves of garlic and 2 tablespoons rock salt or sea salt in the molcajete. Grind with tejolote to make a paste. Cover the surface of the molcajete with the paste and let rest for 30 minutes.

Step 5: Discard garlic paste. In a separate container, make a vinegar and water solution by combining 1 cup white vinegar and 1 cup water. Rinse molcajete with solution and let air-dry completely before using.

Note: Your molcajete will continue to release pieces of rock when used. Don't be surprised if you find little pieces of grit in your salsa.

Totopos Caseros
HOMEMADE TORTILLA CHIPS

There is nothing better to accompany a bowl of salsa than a homemade bowl of tortilla chips! The lure of the crisp, warm, salty crunch when paired with any salsa is one that never gets old. Once you make your own chips, it will be very difficult to enjoy store-bought chips in the same capacity. Plus, they are so easy to make, so why not?
—Nicole

Prep time: 5 minutes
Cook time: 10 minutes
Yields: 4 servings

10 corn tortillas
1 cup vegetable oil

1/2 teaspoon salt, divided

1. Stack tortillas on top of each other; then, with a sharp knife, cut the tortillas into 8 equal triangles (see photo).
2. Heat oil in a large frying pan over a medium-high flame. Attach a frying thermometer to the pan and allow the oil to reach 350 degrees.
3. Drop about 20 triangles at a time into the hot oil. Make sure not to overcrowd the tortillas, as this will not allow them to fry properly. You want them to have a little surrounding space for each chip.
4. Fry on each side for 1 minute; then remove from oil and place on a paper towel–lined plate to drain excess oil.
5. Sprinkle the batch with 1/8 teaspoon salt.
6. Continue frying and salting the tortilla triangles in small batches until finished.
7. Serve warm and enjoy.

   Note: Chips will keep fresh for up to two days.

   Tip: To reheat chips, place in a single layer on a baking sheet and bake for 5 minutes at 200 degrees.

Cooked Salsas

Jalapeños en Salsa Cítrica de Soya

JALAPEÑO SLICES IN CITRUS SOY SAUCE

During our Sunday carne asadas in El Paso, Texas, this spicy, citrusy salsa was front and center on our patio table. Hints of orange and lime, a touch of sweet Worcestershire, umami from the soy sauce, and Maggi seasoning sauce complimented the intense heat of fried jalapeños and serranos.

This tangy and very spicy sauce was the queen of our cookouts because it goes best on tacos de arrachera *or any carne asada dish. Because it packs a big punch, a little goes a long way.*

—Erieka

Prep time: 5 minutes
Cook time: 12 minutes
Yields: 4 cups
Spice level: 🌶🌶🌶

2 tablespoons canola oil
6 serrano chiles, sliced
6 jalapeño chiles, sliced
1 cup sliced white onion
2 cloves of garlic, chopped

1/2 cup fresh orange juice
1/2 cup fresh lime juice
3/4 cup soy sauce
1/4 cup Worcestershire sauce
2 tablespoons Maggi seasoning sauce

1. Heat oil in a large sauté pan over medium heat. Add serranos and jalapeños and increase heat to medium-high. Cook, stirring frequently, for 6 minutes.

2. Add onion and garlic. Continue cooking for 6 minutes or until onion begins to brown. Remove from heat and transfer to a large bowl.

3. Stir in juices, soy sauce, Worcestershire sauce, and Maggi seasoning sauce.

Salsa Cremosa de Aguacate

CREAMY AVOCADO SALSA

This avocado salsa might be creamy, but it sure is the perfect fiery topping for your tacos! Spiced with serrano chiles with the texture of blended avocados, this salsa will always be a guest at your taco table. Make plenty because it will go fast!
—Ericka

Prep time: 10 minutes
Cook time: 15 minutes
Yields: 3 cups
Spice level: 🌶🌶

1/2 tablespoon cooking oil
4 serrano chiles, stems removed
12 tomatillos, husks removed and rinsed
1/4 white onion
3 cloves of garlic

2 large avocados
1 tablespoon lime juice
2 teaspoons sea salt
1 bunch fresh cilantro
3/4 cup water

1. Heat oil in a large frying pan or skillet over medium heat. Add serranos, tomatillos, onion, and garlic.

2. When brown spots begin to appear on onion and garlic, about 5 minutes, remove from pan and add to a blender.

3. Continue frying serranos and tomatillos until char spots form on all sides and tomatillo color has darkened. Transfer to blender.

4. Add avocados, lime juice, salt, cilantro, and water to blender. Blend until smooth.

Nopales Machos

SPICY CACTUS SALSA

Macho—*meaning domineering, proud, and aggressively powerful—is the perfect way to describe these spicy nopales. Mixed with a molcajete paste of fried garlic and dried árbol chiles, these cactus bits can pack an aggressively powerful but delicious punch. The spice can at first be strong, but it will mellow out after the first bite.*
—*Ericka*

Prep time: 15 minutes
Cook time: 35 minutes
Yields: 3 cups
Spice level: ❨❨❨❨

1 pound cactus pads, thorns removed and rinsed
1/3 red onion, sliced
6 cloves of garlic, divided
20 sprigs fresh cilantro
2 teaspoons sea salt, divided

2 teaspoons cooking oil
20 dried árbol chiles, wiped clean
1/2 tablespoon olive oil
1 tablespoon water

1. Chop cactus in small pieces and add to a large saucepan.

2. Add onion, 2 cloves of garlic, cilantro, and 1 teaspoon salt. Place over medium-low heat and cook for 30 minutes.

3. Remove from heat; discard garlic and cilantro. Transfer cactus and onion to a large strainer. Run under cold water to rinse and set aside.

4. Heat cooking oil in a large skillet over medium heat. Add remaining cloves of garlic and lightly fry until dark spots begin to form. Remove garlic from heat and set aside.

5. Add árbol chiles to the skillet and quickly toss to toast, about 15 seconds or until fragrant. Remove from heat and set aside.

6. Place fried cloves of garlic and 1 teaspoon salt in a molcajete (or mortar and pestle). Crush until a paste forms.

7. Add fried árbol chiles and crush into flakes.

8. Stir in olive oil and water.

9. Add cactus mixture and stir to coat evenly with chile flakes.

Salsa de Pasilla y Chile de Árbol

PASILLA AND ÁRBOL CHILE SALSA

This pasilla and árbol chile salsa is my fajita salsa of choice. Whether your sizzling fajitas are chicken, beef, or mushroom, nothing else goes better with them than this sauce. Don't have time to make fajitas? Fry some panela or halloumi cheese, wrap it in a corn tortilla, and sprinkle this sauce on top. I promise you are going to love it!

—Ericka

Prep time: 10 minutes
Cook time: 15 minutes
Yields: 2 3/4 cups
Spice level:

3 tablespoons cooking oil
3/4 cup roughly chopped white onion
2 large cloves of garlic
16 dried árbol chiles, stems removed
4 dried pasilla chiles, stems and seeds removed

4 tomatillos, sliced in half
1 cup water
1 1/2 teaspoons sea salt
1 1/4 cups chopped cilantro, divided

1. Heat oil in a large cast-iron skillet over medium heat. Add onion and garlic. Cook for 3 minutes, stirring frequently.

2. Add dried chiles and tomatillos. Cook for 3 minutes; then add water. Simmer for 4 minutes or until tomatillos begin to darken in color.

3. Transfer to blender; add salt and 1 cup cilantro. Blend for 20 seconds.

4. Heat the same skillet over medium heat. Pour in salsa and simmer for 5 minutes. Transfer to a serving bowl and stir in remaining cilantro.

Salsa Asada de Tomatillo
ROASTED GREEN TOMATILLO SALSA

The depth and flavor of this roasted green tomatillo salsa is released the more you crush and grind with the tejolote. It's chunky, smoky, and so delicious—perfect to accompany just about every meal! Make a few batches and freeze so you'll never run out.
—*Ericka*

Prep time: 30 minutes
Cook time: 20 minutes
Yields: 2 cups
Spice level: 🌶🌶

1 pound tomatillos, husks removed and rinsed
1/3 white onion
1 large jalapeño chile
3 serrano chiles

3 cloves of garlic, unpeeled, divided
1 tablespoon sea salt
1/3 cup fresh cilantro, roughly chopped

1. Place tomatillos, onion, jalapeño, serranos, and 2 cloves of garlic on a large cast-iron skillet over medium-high heat. Roast, turning frequently with tongs, until dark char spots appear evenly on all sides. Tomatillos should be yellowish in color and soft.

2. Set garlic aside and place charred tomatillos, onion, and chiles in a zip bag. Seal and let contents steam and cool for 15 minutes.

3. While steaming, peel all cloves of garlic. Add garlic and salt to a molcajete. Grind until cloves break apart and a paste forms.

4. Add onion and grind until it breaks apart and becomes part of the paste.

5. Destem chiles and add to the molcajete. Grind until chiles break apart.

6. Add cilantro and grind until it becomes part of the paste.

7. Add tomatillos, two to three at a time, to the molcajete. Pierce tomatillos a few times with a knife and crush with tejolote to break up. Repeat with remaining tomatillos.

8. Continue crushing and grinding until desired consistency.

9. Add any remaining liquid from the bag the ingredients steamed in and stir.

Salsa Classica Molcajeteada

CLASSIC MOLCAJETE SALSA

Here it is! The salsa of all salsas! This is the salsa I picture when I think of the word "salsa" and the only salsa I would learn to make if I had a choice of learning how to make just one. The flavor and texture from the molcajete are what gives this salsa its distinctive classic taste. It's also a great salsa to break in your new molcajete.

—Ericka

Prep time: 20 minutes
Cook time: 15 minutes
Yields: 3 cups
Spice level: 𝄃𝄃𝄃

5 small Roma tomatoes, stem scars removed
1 large tomatillo, stem scar removed
1/4 white onion, sliced in half
1 large jalapeño chile, stem removed

2 serrano chiles, stems removed
3 cloves of garlic, unpeeled
1 1/2 teaspoons sea salt
1/3 cup fresh cilantro, roughly chopped

1. Place tomatoes, tomatillo, onion, chiles, and garlic on a large comal (or skillet) over medium heat.

2. Remove cloves of garlic as soon as char spots appear. Let cool and peel.

3. Roast tomatoes, tomatillo, onion, and chiles until char spots form and tomatoes begin to break apart.

4. Add salt and cloves of garlic to a molcajete. Crush with tejolote until a paste forms.

5. Add onion and crush until onion breaks down and a thick paste forms.

6. Add chiles. Pierce with a paring knife; then crush into small pieces.

7. Add tomatoes and tomatillo and crush until desired consistency.

8. Stir in cilantro and serve with chips or tostadas.

ROASTED CHEESE SALSA

Salsa de queso asado, *roasted cheese salsa, is my favorite to serve for breakfast. Slices of queso fresco are added to this salsa because the cheese is salty and softens without melting. Because the cheese keeps its shape, it roasts and grills perfectly, creating a delicious, charred crust that incorporates with roasted Roma tomatoes, spicy chiles, and onion pieces.*
—*Ericka*

Prep time: 10 minutes
Cook time: 25 minutes
Yields: 2 cups
Spice level:

2 large Roma tomatoes, cored

2 large jalapeño chiles, stems removed

1 large serrano chile, stem removed

1/3 white onion, roughly chopped in 2-inch pieces

2 teaspoons cooking oil

1 wheel (10 ounces) queso fresco, sliced in 1/2-inch x 2-inch slices

1. Place tomatoes, chiles, and onion on a cast-iron skillet or comal over medium-high heat. Turn frequently with tongs until dark char spots appear on all sides.

2. Transfer to a molcajete or large bowl. Crush with tejolote or potato masher until a chunky texture forms. Set aside.

3. Heat oil in a large non-stick pan over medium heat. Add 3–4 cheese slices to the pan, leaving 2 inches between each slice. Cook for 3 minutes on each side or until cheese chars. Transfer to salsa bowl. Repeat until all cheese slices are roasted.

4. Serve with tortillas or breakfast eggs.

Salsa Macha
MEXICAN CHILE OIL

Salsa macha—a smoky, deep, and complex flavor with an array of a nutty mixture—is what makes this one of my favorite salsas. Not only does this delicious sauce last for months, but it also goes with just about any meal—from breakfast eggs to carne asada tacos to a drizzle on your salads and soups.

—Ericka

Prep time: 10 minutes
Cook time: 20 minutes
Yields: 1 3/4 cups
Spice level: ꓲꓲꓲꓲ

1/4 cup sesame seeds
3 tablespoons raw pine nuts
1/4 cup raw peanuts, shelled
3 tablespoons raw pepitas

1 cup + 2 tablespoons cooking oil, divided
5 cloves of garlic
3 cups dried árbol chiles, stems removed

1. Toast sesame seeds in a large pan over low-medium heat for about 2 minutes, stirring frequently, or until seeds change to a golden-brown color. Transfer to a medium bowl.

2. Add pine nuts to pan and toast for 2–3 minutes, stirring frequently, or until golden-brown spots appear. Transfer to the bowl with sesame seeds.

3. Add peanuts to pan and toast for 3 minutes, stirring frequently, or until golden brown. Transfer to the bowl with sesame seeds and pine nuts.

4. Add pepitas to pan and toast for 2 minutes, stirring frequently, or until golden brown. Transfer to the bowl with seeds and nuts. Stir to mix and set aside.

5. Heat 2 tablespoons cooking oil over medium heat. Add garlic and fry until golden brown, about 2 minutes, stirring frequently. Transfer fried garlic to a food processor or blender.

6. Add remaining oil to pan and heat. Add árbol chiles and fry, stirring frequently, for 45–60 seconds. Do not burn. Let oil cool before adding it and the chiles to the food processor.

7. Add 3 tablespoons seed and nut mixture to the food processor. Blend for 1 minute or until smooth.

8. Transfer to a serving bowl, add the remaining seed and nut mixture, and stir.

Salsa Martajada con Aguacate
CHUNKY SALSA WITH AVOCADO

Any salsa with chunks of avocado has my attention. This chunky salsa is my favorite salsa for skirt steak tacos or to serve with crispy tortilla chips. It's tangy with creamy avocado bits and the right amount of spice.
—*Ericka*

Prep time: 15 minutes
Cook time: 10 minutes
Yields: 2 cups
Spice level: 𝄫

5 large tomatillos
2 serrano chiles
1 jalapeño chile
1 large clove of garlic

1 teaspoon chicken bouillon
1/3 cup diced white onion
1/4 cup diced fresh cilantro
3/4 cup chopped avocado

1. Combine tomatillos, serranos, and jalapeño in a large saucepan with enough water to cover them. Heat over medium heat. When water begins to boil, turn heat off and let tomatillos and chiles continue to cook until tomatillos darken in color. Remove from water and slice off chile stems.

2. Combine tomatillos, serranos, jalapeño, garlic, and bouillon in a blender. Pulse a few times for a chunky consistency. Transfer to a serving bowl and let cool.

3. Once cooled, stir in onion, cilantro, and avocado.

Salsa de Aguacate sin Aguacate

NO AVOCADO-AVOCADO SAUCE

If you've visited a Mexican taqueria in the last decade or two, you've probably been fooled by this "avocado" salsa. Well, the secret is out—it's been discovered that this creamy salsa does not contain avocado at all! Give it a try.
—Ericka

Prep time: 10 minutes
Cook time: 15 minutes
Yields: 2 1/2 cups
Spice level: 🌶

3 large Mexican zucchinis, cut in thick slices
8 tomatillos
2 tablespoons cooking oil
2 large jalapeño chiles, stems removed and halved lengthwise

1/3 cup sliced white onion
2 large cloves of garlic
1/3 cup fresh cilantro
1 tablespoon chicken or vegetable bouillon

1. Add zucchini and tomatillos to a large saucepan and cover them with water. Remove from heat when tomatillos darken in color. Drain and transfer to a blender.

2. While zucchini and tomatillos cook, heat oil in a large skillet over medium heat. Add jalapeños and onion. Cook for 3 minutes or until onions are lightly fried. Transfer to a blender.

3. Fry garlic until golden brown, about 1 minute. Transfer to blender.

4. Add cilantro and bouillon to blender. Blend until smooth.

MEXICAN BLISTERED CHILES

The first time I had chiles toreados was at a busy taco stand in Mexicali, Mexico, in the wee hours of the morning. The small border town serves up these pan-fried blistered Güero chiles alongside a plate of tacos or quesadillas. They are super flavorful and pack the perfect amount of heat. Some people use this exact method of cooking with jalapeños instead, but I am partial to the yellow Güero chile because it allows the tanginess of the lime to shine through a little more.

—Nicole

Prep time: 5 minutes
Cook time: 15 minutes
Yields: 10 chiles
Spice level: 🌶🌶🌶

10 Güero chiles
2 tablespoons vegetable oil
2 tablespoons soy sauce

1/4 cup lime juice
1/8 teaspoon salt

1. Rinse chiles under cold water to clean them and then dry them with a paper towel.
2. Cut a small slit (1/4-inch) on one side of each chile with a paring knife; this will keep them from busting open during the cooking process.
3. Heat vegetable oil in a large frying pan over a medium-high heat.
4. Arrange chiles in the frying pan and cook for 10 minutes or until all sides of chiles are browned, turning every 2 minutes.
5. Drizzle soy sauce and lime juice over frying chiles; then cover the pan with a lid and lower heat to medium-low to allow chiles to steam for 5 minutes.
6. Remove chiles from pan and sprinkle with salt.

Salsa Taquera
TACO SAUCE

Salsa taquera *makes me super happy when drizzled over tacos. This is the salsa you eat with caution at first because it looks super spicy, but you continue to add more after each bite because the taste is just right! It pairs really well with a carne asada burrito too.*
—*Nicole*

Prep time: 10 minutes
Cook time: 15 minutes
Yields: 4 cups
Spice level: 𝄞𝄞𝄞

1 1/2 pounds Milpero tomatillos
3 cloves of garlic
1 teaspoon salt
2 chipotle peppers in adobo sauce
1 tablespoon adobo sauce

1/2 cup water
15 chiles tepín
1/2 cup chopped cilantro
1/2 cup chopped onion

1.   Remove husks from tomatillos and rinse under cold water to remove any debris.

2.   Roast tomatillos and cloves of garlic on a hot comal over medium-high heat. The garlic will roast in 5 minutes; remove when completely browned. The tomatillos will take 10–15 minutes.

3.   Add roasted tomatillos, garlic, salt, chipotle peppers, adobo sauce, water, and chiles tepín to a blender and blend for 1 minute.

4.   Remove mixture from blender and fold in chopped cilantro and onion.

5.   Serve hot or cold.

Salsa Sencilla
SIMPLE SALSA

I think of this as a backyard salsa. The kind that shows up at every carne asada gathering. It's conventional in the sense that it can be topped on a variety of dishes and is a mainstay of the salsa family, maybe because of its no-fuss preparation leads to one of the tastiest salsas out there, with a fine balance between the tomatoes, árbol chiles, jalapeño, and raw garlic. I think you'll love it.
—*Nicole*

Prep time: 5 minutes
Cook time: 25 minutes
Yields: 2 cups
Spice level:

1 jalapeño chile
3 árbol chiles
5 Roma tomatoes

3 cloves of garlic
1 teaspoon salt

1. Fill a pot halfway with water and place over a high heat; bring to a boil.

2. Add jalapeño, árbol chiles, and tomatoes.

3. Boil for 25 minutes or until the tomatoes can be pierced with a fork.

4. Drain tomatoes and chiles.

5. Remove stems from chiles.

6. Place all ingredients in a blender and pulse 10 times or until all ingredients are combined and just slightly chunky.

7. Serve warm or cold.

    Tip: You can store this salsa in a glass jar; it will keep in the refrigerator for up to a week.

Salsa de Pimiento Rojo
SMOKY RED PEPPER SALSA

The first time I had this salsa it was made tableside at a restaurant in Mexico City. I was fascinated that the main ingredient was roasted red bell pepper (the kind you can buy in a jar) instead of tomato and then perfumed with a touch of smoky spice. I have since recreate this recipe at home dozens of times and love how flavorful it is.

—Nicole

Prep time: 10 minutes
Grind time: 20 minutes
Yields: 2 cups
Spice level:

7 tablespoons olive oil
1 medium white onion, diced
1 teaspoon salt
14 pequín chiles

5 cloves of garlic
1 cup roasted red bell pepper
1/2 cup lime juice

1. Add 2 tablespoons olive oil to a small frying pan over medium heat and allow to get hot. Add diced onion and sauté for 7–10 minutes or until onions are translucent, mixing occasionally. Set aside until ready to use.

2. Add salt, pequín chiles, and garlic to a molcajete. Using a tejolote, grind the ingredients into a paste.

3. Grind in onion until it is incorporated into the paste.

4. Add roasted bell pepper and continue grinding until pureed. This takes some serious arm work!

5. Pour in olive oil and lime juice. Mix vigorously to combine.

6. Serve with warm corn chips.

Salsa de Tamarindo
TAMARIND SALSA

This spicy-sweet salsa is perfect dolloped in ceviche or drizzled over chicken or carnitas! Feel free to double or triple the recipe to make a larger batch for big parties or gatherings.

—Nicole

Prep time: 10 minutes
Cook time: 30 minutes
Yields: 1 cup
Spice level:

10 tamarind rods
1 habanero chile, stem removed
4 cloves of garlic
1 tablespoon ginger

1/2 teaspoon salt
2 tablespoons olive oil
1 tablespoon brown sugar
1 tablespoon honey or agave

1. Peel and devein tamarind rods. Place sticky inner flesh in a pot of boiling water. Boil until soft, about 30 minutes. Allow to cool to room temperature. Remove seeds from flesh. Reserve 1/3 cup tamarind water for later use.

2. Brown habanero, garlic, and ginger on a comal or griddle until soft and aroma intensifies, about 5–7 minutes. Garlic will brown the fastest in about 3 minutes.

3. Blend the tamarind pulp, tamarind water, habanero, garlic, ginger, salt, olive oil, brown sugar, and honey/agave until smooth.

Fresh Salsas

Salsa Verde Cruda
FRESH GREEN SALSA

I'm a big fan of tomatillos in any shape or form. But my favorite way to enjoy them in the summertime is in a fresh salsa verde cruda. *This delicious salsa comes together in just a few minutes and goes great over tacos, eggs, grilled fish, and carne asada. It's a great way to pack a punch to your dishes with minimal effort.*
—Ericka

Prep time: 10 minutes
Yields: 1 3/4 cups
Spice level:

1/2 pound tomatillos, husked, rinsed, and roughly chopped
1/3 cup roughly chopped white onion
4 serrano chiles, stems removed and roughly chopped
1/3 cup fresh cilantro

1 sprig mint
1/3 cup water
1 teaspoon sea salt

1. Add all ingredients to blender. Pulse to a chunky consistency.

2. Pour into a salsa bowl and serve.

Salsa Bandera
PICO DE GALLO

Some people call this traditional taco topper pico de gallo, *but I've also known it as* salsa bandera *for its colors of the Mexican flag: red, white, and green. Whatever you choose to call it, just make sure you have plenty in the house whenever it's time to eat!*
—*Nicole*

Prep time: 15 minutes
Yields: 4 1/2 cups
Spice level: 🌶🌶

3 cups Roma tomatoes, chopped
1/2 teaspoon garlic powder
1 1/2 teaspoons salt
1/4 cup lime juice

1/2 large white onion
1 1/2 large jalapeño chiles
1/2 cup cilantro leaves

1. Place tomatoes in a bowl with garlic powder, salt, and lime juice. Allow to marinade while you prep the remaining ingredients.

2. Chop the onion.

3. Dice the jalapeños.

4. Mix onion, jalapeños, and cilantro into the marinating tomatoes.

Xnipec

DOG'S NOSE

Pronounced "shnee-peck"—from the Mayan word ni, *meaning "nose," and* peek, *meaning "dog"—this salsa is called "dog's nose" because it is so spicy it will make your nose sweat. Just like a dog's nose. With bits of tomato, red onion, cilantro, and chile, all finely chopped and salted, it is similar to pico de gallo. The difference: the chile used is habanero and the entire salsa is then mixed with sour orange juice (or a combination of orange and lime juices). Use gloves when chopping! This is a very popular salsa in the Yucatán Peninsula and is used to accompany most of their dishes.*

—Ericka

Prep time: 10 minutes
Chill time: 4 hours
Yields: 2 cups
Spice level: 🌶🌶🌶🌶🌶

3 habanero chiles, stems, seeds, and veins removed; diced

1 1/3 cups Roma tomatoes, chopped

3/4 cup red onion, chopped

3 tablespoons fresh cilantro, finely chopped

2 tablespoons fresh lime juice

2 tablespoons fresh orange juice

1/2 teaspoon sea salt

1.   Combine all ingredients except salt in a medium bowl. Toss to mix well, cover, and refrigerate for 4 hours.

2.   Fold in salt before serving.

Salsa de Xoconostle
XOCONOSTLE SALSA

Xoconostle is a tasty, tart cactus fruit that makes a delicious salsa and margarita! Because the fruit is nice and tangy, no lime juice is needed, just plenty of elbow grease because most of this salsa's ingredients will be ground up in a molcajete. Xoconostle can be found at your Latin supermarket. The fruit can be easily confused with prickly pears; if you are not sure, ask the produce manager for clarification.
—Ericka

Prep time: 15 minutes
Yields: 1 3/4 cups
Spice level:

1/2 teaspoon sea salt
1 small clove of garlic
4 serrano chiles, roughly chopped
5 xoconostles

1/4 white onion, diced
1 large Roma tomato, diced
1/3 cup cilantro, chopped

1. Combine salt and garlic in a molcajete. Mash until a paste forms.

2. Add serranos and mash into small pieces.

3. Carefully peel each xoconostle using a paring knife. Slice the fruit lengthwise and scoop out and discard as many seeds as possible. Add the fruit flesh to the molcajete and mash into a chunky paste.

4. Stir in onion, tomato, and cilantro. Serve immediately.

Chile de Árbol Salsa Brava
ÁRBOL CHILE HOT SAUCE

This hot sauce comes together in minutes because none of the ingredients need to be heated. Unless your tongue craves fire, this salsa is best eaten in small amounts because it is super spicy. Enjoy on soft tacos, add a few drops to soup, or squirt over nachos!
—Nicole

Prep time: 5 minutes
Yields: 2 1/2 cups
Spice level: (((((

1 1/2 cups árbol chiles, stems removed
4 Roma tomatoes
1 cup water
4 cloves of garlic

2 small limes or 1 large lime, juiced
1 teaspoon salt
2 teaspoons white vinegar

1. Add all ingredients to a blender and blend until smooth.

2. Pour salsa mixture through a sieve and into a bowl. Press chile flesh and seeds against sieve with the back of a spoon to squeeze out all liquid. Discard any seeds and skin collected in sieve.

Enchilada Sauces

Salsa para Enchiladas Rojas

RED ENCHILADA SAUCE

This is my tried-and-true sauce for enchiladas rojas. *It's classic and brings the taste of many memorable meals to my palate. I hope you'll enjoy it too!*
—Nicole

Prep time: 10 minutes
Cook time: 40 minutes
Yields: 6 1/2 cups
Spice level: 🌶🌶

2 1/2 ounces New Mexico chiles
2 1/2 ounces California chiles
1 ounce pasilla-ancho chiles
2 ounces guajillo chiles

5 cups water
1 tablespoon + 1 teaspoon salt, divided
1 medium white onion
5 cloves of garlic

1. Wipe down all chiles with a damp cloth to remove any dirt particles.

2. Heat a comal over a medium-high heat and toast the chiles for 1 minute on each side. Remove from comal.

3. Add water and 1 tablespoon salt to a large pot; bring to a boil. Add toasted chiles and onion. Boil for 35–40 minutes or until chiles soften. Reserve boiled chile water for later steps.

4. Remove chiles from water and discard stems.

5. Place chile skins, 3 cups boiled chile water, onion, and garlic in a blender. Blend until smooth.

6. Pour chile sauce mixture through a sieve and into a bowl. Press chile flesh against sieve to squeeze out all liquid. Discard any seeds and skin collected in sieve.

7. Stir in 1 teaspoon salt and 1 cup chile water. Mix to combine.

   Tip: This sauce can be stored in an airtight container for up to a week in the refrigerator.

   Tip: This sauce can also be used in a batch of chilaquiles.

Salsa para Enchiladas Verdes
GREEN ENCHILADA SAUCE

Green enchiladas are the gateway to a perfect meal. For me, it's all about the sauce you pour over the rolled fried tortillas. This green enchilada sauce is so tasty you can pour it over any stuffed tortilla and have a meal you will crave again and again.
—*Nicole*

Prep time: 10 minutes
Cook time: 30 minutes
Yields: 8 cups
Spice level: (((

4 Anaheim chiles
1 tablespoon oil
8 large tomatillos, husks removed and rinsed
2 serrano chiles, stems removed
1/3 cup roughly chopped onion

2 cloves of garlic
4 cups chicken or vegetable broth
3/4 cup cilantro
1 tablespoon salt
6 peppercorns

1. Roast Anaheim chiles over an open flame until charred. This should take about 10 minutes. Place in an airtight bag to sweat for 20 minutes.

2. While the Anaheim chiles are sweating, add oil to a large frying pan over medium-high heat. Add tomatillos, serranos, and onion to pan. Sauté in oil for 5 minutes or until spotted.

3. Add garlic and continue to brown for 5 minutes.

4. Pour in broth and allow mixture to simmer for 20 minutes on low.

5. Remove Anaheim chiles from bag and remove stems and charred skin by scraping the chiles with a butter knife.

6. Add all ingredients to a blender and blend until smooth.

Tip: The alternative to Roasting Chiles instead of over an open flame can be done in an oven. Preheat oven to 425 degrees and roast on a baking sheet for 15 minutes or until chiles blister.

Sweet and Spicy Salsas

Salsa de Mango y Habanero

MANGO HABANERO SALSA

This mango habanero salsa is the perfect balance of sweet and spicy. The heat is quite high but mellows out almost instantly. With the tanginess of vinegar, lime juice, and a touch of ginger, this salsa makes a great dipping sauce and marinade for shrimp, chicken wings, or beef. It makes a great make-ahead salsa to liven up any meal. Make sure to store it in an airtight glass container and refrigerate until use.
—*Ericka*

Prep time: 10 minutes
Cook time: 15 minutes
Yields: 1 3/4 cups
Spice level: ((((

2 habanero chiles
2 cloves of garlic, unpeeled
1/4 white onion
1 1/2 cups mango pulp
1 tablespoon sugar
1 tablespoon lime juice

1 teaspoon Worcestershire sauce
1/4 cup white vinegar
1/2 teaspoon chopped fresh ginger
1/4 teaspoon sea salt
1/2 cup water

1. Place habaneros, garlic, and onion on a comal or skillet over medium heat. Use tongs to roast evenly on all sides until charred spots form.

2. Remove garlic from heat and peel.

3. Slice stems off habaneros.

4. Combine all ingredients in a blender or a food processor. Blend until smooth.

5. Serve or use as a marinade.

Salsa de Flor de Jamaica

HIBISCUS BLOOM SALSA

Whenever you are making agua de Jamaica *(hibiscus beverage), don't discard the blooms. Make this tasty, piquant concoction to go along with your tortilla chips. With four different types of dried red chiles, this salsa packs a punch. Spice aficionados will love it!*
—*Ericka*

Prep time: 10 minutes
Cook time: 15 minutes
Yields: 2 cups
Spice level: ❮❮❮

2 cups dried hibiscus blooms, rinsed and drained
4 cups water
1 tablespoon cooking oil
3 large cloves of garlic
4 dried morita chiles

1 guajillo chile, stem removed
1 puya chile, stem removed
20 árbol chiles, stems removed
1 1/2 tablespoons granulated sugar
1 teaspoon sea salt

1. Combine hibiscus blooms and water in a large saucepan over medium heat. Bring to a boil. Remove from heat and let blooms hydrate for 10 minutes.

2. While blooms hydrate, heat oil in a large frying pan over medium-low heat. Lightly fry garlic until golden brown. Transfer to blender.

3. In the same frying pan, add morita, guajillo, puya, and árbol chiles. Quickly fry, stirring constantly to avoid burning, about 1 minute. Transfer all chiles to blender.

4. Drain hibiscus blooms, reserving 1 cup of the liquid. Add blooms, reserved water, sugar, and salt to blender. Blend for 15 seconds or until desired consistency.

5. Transfer to a salsa bowl and serve with corn tortilla chips.

Salsa de Piña a la Parrilla
GRILLED PINEAPPLE SALSA

Grilled pineapple is delicious as an addition to any habanero-spiced salsas. Next time your grill is on, toss a pineapple slice over the grill, chop it up, and add it to a mixture of onion, habaneros, cilantro, and avocado. This medley is a must for any seafood dish, especially fish tacos. Yum!
—Ericka

Prep time: 10 minutes
Cook time: 10 minutes
Yields: 2 cups
Spice level:

1 pineapple slice, 1-inch thick
2 green onions, sliced
1/4 cup chopped red onion
2 habanero chiles, sliced
1/3 cup cilantro, finely chopped
1/2 teaspoon sea salt

2 teaspoons Worcestershire sauce
2 teaspoons Maggi seasoning sauce
2 tablespoons lime juice
1 tablespoon olive oil
1 cup chopped avocado

1. Place pineapple slice on the grill over medium-high heat. Grill on both sides until char marks appear. Remove from heat, let cool, and chop.

2. Combine grilled pineapple chunks, green onions, red onion, habaneros, and cilantro in a medium bowl.

3. Add salt, Worcestershire sauce, Maggi seasoning sauce, lime juice, and olive oil. Stir to mix well.

4. Fold in avocado chunks and serve immediately.

Chamoy Casero
HOMEMADE CHAMOY

You will never use store-bought chamoy after you make this delicious, sweet, tangy, and spicy chamoy sauce at home. Chamoy makes a great fruit topping and rim sauce for your favorite cocktails and fruit slushies.
—Ericka

Prep time: 10 minutes
Cook time: 35 minutes
Yields: 2 1/2 cups
Spice level: 🌶

1 cup dried apricots
1/2 cup prunes
3/4 cup dried hibiscus blooms, rinsed and drained
3 1/2 cups water

1/2 cup granulated sugar
1/4 cup Tajín Clásico Seasoning
1 tablespoon árbol chile powder
1/4 cup fresh lime juice

1. Combine apricots, prunes, hibiscus, water, sugar, Tajín, and chile powder in a large saucepan over medium heat. Simmer for 35 minutes. Remove from heat and let cool.

2. Transfer everything in the saucepan to a blender. Add lime juice and blend until completely smooth. Transfer to a jar. Refrigerate when not using.

Salsa de Mango y Aguacate
MANGO AVOCADO SALSA

Cold, fruity salsa is best enjoyed with a pile of chips. This mango avocado salsa has a little bit of a sweet bite in between the creamy avocado chunks, leaving you with a mouth full of yum and wanting more.
—Nicole

Prep time: 20 minutes
Chill time: 1 hour
Yields: 3 cups
Spice level:

3 tablespoons minced jalapeño chiles
2 Roma tomatoes, cut in 1/4-inch cubes
1 teaspoon salt
1/2 teaspoon garlic powder
1/2 teaspoon chile flakes
1/4 cup lime juice
1/4 cup orange or mango juice

1 teaspoon olive oil
1/3 cup cilantro leaves
1 cup diced red onion
1 1/2 cups diced mango
1 1/2 cups diced avocado
1 teaspoon hot sauce

1. Combine all ingredients in a bowl. Mix well and place in refrigerator for 1 hour to chill and allow flavors to marinate together.

2. Serve cold with chips.

Salsa de Fresa y Serrano
STRAWBERRY SERRANO SALSA

This is the ultimate summer pico de gallo. Make it when strawberries are at the height of their sweetness. The combination of sweet with spicy is a great topper for grilled fish tacos or as a snack to accompany a glass of chilled rosé wine. I like to use a combination of serrano chiles and roasted pasilla chiles to even out the heat.
—Nicole

Prep time: 5 minutes
Rest time: 20 minutes
Yields: 2 1/2 cups
Spice level: ❮❮❮

1 1/2 cups diced strawberries
1/4 cup fresh lime juice
1/2 cup chopped cilantro leaves
2 1/2 serrano chiles, minced

1 cup diced red onion
1 pasilla chile, roasted, peeled, and chopped
1/2 teaspoon salt

1. Mix all ingredients in a bowl and allow to rest for 20 minutes. This will give the flavors a chance to infuse with one another.

2. Serve with chips and enjoy!

Curtidos and Escabeches

Curtido de Cebolla y Chile Pequín

PICKLED ONIONS WITH PEQUÍN CHILE

Serve this elevated version of pickled onions on your tacos, sandwiches, quesadillas, salads, and even cheese boards. Dripping in spicy lime juice with a touch of cilantro, these pickled onions with chile pequín *will be a mealtime staple.*

—Ericka

Prep time: 15 minutes
Yields: 2 1/2 cups
Spice level: 🌶🌶🌶

2 tablespoons dried pequín chiles
4 dried árbol chiles, stems removed
2 cloves of garlic
2 red jalapeño chiles, stems removed, sliced
1 teaspoon salt

1 large red onion, sliced
1 cup lime juice
1/3 cup olive oil
3/4 cup cilantro sprigs, chopped

1. Place pequín chiles, árbol chiles, and garlic in a large molcajete. Mash into a coarse paste.

2. Add jalapeños and salt and mash until jalapeño slices break up into small pieces.

3. Add onion, lime juice, and olive oil to the molcajete. Toss to distribute ingredients evenly.

4. Stir in cilantro. Serve immediately or store in an airtight glass container in the refrigerator.

Curtido de Jicama Zanahoria y Pepino

JICAMA, CARROT, AND CUCUMBER CURTIDO

On your tostadas, tacos, pupusas, arepas, or gorditas, this jicama, carrot, and cucumber curtido is a delicious, crunchy topping. Full of tangy flavor with a tasty crunch, your meals won't be the same without it. It is great for summer cookouts and picnics.
—Erieka

Prep time: 10 minutes
Chill time: 1 hour
Yields: 3 3/4 cups
Spice level: 🌙

1 cup shredded jicama
1 cup shredded carrots
1 cup diced cucumber
1/4 cup sliced red onion
1 jalapeño chile, diced

1 serrano chile, diced
1/3 cup chopped cilantro
1 tablespoon lime juice
1 tablespoon olive oil
1/2 teaspoon sea salt

1. Toss all ingredients together in a medium bowl.

2. Cover and refrigerate for 1 hour. Serve chilled.

Curtido
CABBAGE SLAW

Cabbage curtido brings the crunch to any pupusa. This tangy cabbage slaw is a bit sour, sweet, and spicy. I pile it on my pupusas, but welcome it as a fresh condiment on top of tacos too!
—*Nicole*

Prep time: 15 minutes
Rest time: 1 hour
Chill time: Overnight
Yields: 5 1/2 cups
Spice level:

4 cups shredded cabbage
1/2 cup grated carrot
1/2 cup thinly sliced onion
1 small jalapeño chile, seeds removed, minced
1/2 cup apple cider vinegar

1/4 cup water
1 teaspoon salt
1 teaspoon brown sugar
1 teaspoon oregano
1 teaspoon dried pepper flakes

1. Mix cabbage, carrot, onion, and jalapeños together in a large mixing bowl.

2. Whisk apple cider vinegar, water, salt, brown sugar, oregano, and dried pepper flakes together in a small saucepan over medium-low heat. Heat until sugar is dissolved.

3. Pour vinegar mixture over cabbage-onion mixture.

4. Bring to room temperature, at least 1 hour; then cover bowl and place in the refrigerator overnight to rest.

Chiles Curtidos
PICKLED CHILES

It's nice to have a jar of pickled jalapeños in the refrigerator for any spur-of-the-moment craving. They go perfectly with a plate of tacos or chopped up in a tuna salad. I even mix them into my homemade sourdough bread! They are remarkably easy to make and keep in the refrigerator for up to two months.

—Nicole

Prep time: 5 minutes
Cook time: 25 minutes
Rest time: 1 hour
Yields: 20 servings
Spice level: 🌶🌶🌶

1 cup olive oil
4 carrots, peeled and cut into 1/2-inch rounds
1 large white onion, sliced
8 cloves of garlic
20 jalapeño chiles, each punctured with 2 small slits
Black pepper, to taste

1 tablespoon salt
1 teaspoon oregano
2 cups white vinegar
2 cups water
3 bay leaves

1. Heat olive oil over medium-high heat in a large pot.

2. Sauté carrots and onion for 3 minutes or until the onion becomes translucent and the carrots turn a bright orange color; then add garlic and continue to sauté for 1 minute. Remove carrots, onion, and garlic from the oil and set aside.

3. In the same oil, sauté jalapeños for 3 minutes or until the skin starts to wilt and slightly blister. Add the carrots, onion, and garlic back into the pot and mix to combine.

4. Add pepper, salt, oregano, vinegar, water, and bay leaves and simmer for 10–15 minutes.

5. Remove from heat and allow to cool to room temperature, at least 1 hour. Store in a glass jar or plastic container; can keep up to 2 months in the refrigerator.

   Tip: Making two small slits in each chile will keep them from exploding during the frying process, as well as allow the vinegar to soak through more easily.

Moles and Pipianes

GREEN PIPIAN

Pipian verde, *also known as* mole verde, *is one of the more simple moles to prepare without sacrificing any flavor. This beyond delicious, savory green mole comes together in just about an hour. It can be used to make* enmoladas, *paired with your favorite protein (chicken, turkey, seafood), or simply poured over white rice and vegetables. There is no wrong way to eat it! It is so good it may just become a staple in your house, as it is in mine.*

—*Nicole*

Prep time: 15 minutes
Cook time: 1 hour
Yields: 7 cups
Spice level:

2 tablespoons olive oil, divided
3 cups tomatillos, husked, rinsed, and chopped
1 1/3 cups chopped white onion
2 cloves of garlic
1/2 cup pepitas
1/2 cup peanuts, shelled
2 tablespoons sesame seeds
2 cups poblano chiles, seeds removed, diced

1/4 cup serrano chiles, seeds removed, diced
1 cup radish leaves, stems removed
1 cup chopped lettuce leaves
2 corn tortillas, cut into pieces
15 black peppercorns
1 teaspoon salt
4 cups broth—vegetable, chicken, or fish

1. Heat 1 tablespoon olive oil in a large skillet over a medium heat until hot.

2. Sauté tomatillos, onion, and garlic in oil for about 7 minutes or until tomatillos go from a bright green to a pale green and are slightly browned.

3. Remove with slotted spoon and place in blender.

4. In the same large skillet, heat 1/2 tablespoon olive oil and roast pepitas, peanuts, and sesame seeds in skillet for 3 minutes, mixing constantly so they don't burn.

5. Remove with slotted spoon and place in blender.

6. In the same large skillet, heat 1/2 tablespoon olive oil and sauté poblano and serrano chiles for 5 minutes.

7. Add radish leaves, lettuce, and tortillas and sauté for 3 minutes; then add peppercorns, salt, and broth.

8. Bring to a boil (takes about 5 minutes).

9. Pour into blender and blend until smooth, about 1 minute.

10. Pour mixture back into skillet and allow to simmer over a low heat for 30 minutes.

Pipian Rojo
RED PIPIAN

Pipian rojo, or red pipian, is made with three types of dried chiles and a variety of seeds and nuts. The flavor is smoky and nutty, and has a late kick that makes you want more and more. It's great drizzled over fried eggs or totopos—*chilaquiles style—or served in a more formal dinner setting with cooked chicken, turkey, or shrimp. Plate with rice for the perfect meal pairing.*
—Ericka

Prep time: 30 minutes
Cook time: 50 minutes
Yields: 2 1/2 cups
Spice level: 🌙

3 large Roma tomatoes
6 black peppercorns
6 whole allspice
4 whole cloves
1 cinnamon stick
1/8 teaspoon whole cumin
1 1/4 cups raw pepitas, divided
6 tablespoons sesame seeds, divided
1/3 cup + 1/4 cup raw peanuts, shelled, divided
1/2 cup cooking oil, divided

4 cloves of garlic
1/3 onion, chopped into 1-inch pieces
2 slices day-old bolillo
2 dried morita chiles, wiped clean
2 dried chipotle chiles, wiped clean
3 dried ancho chiles, wiped clean and seeds removed
1 cup water
4 cups chicken broth
3 teaspoons salt or chicken bouillon

1. Roast tomatoes on a skillet or comal over medium heat. Using tongs, turn frequently until the tomatoes soften and skin begins to peel off. Set aside.

2. Toast peppercorns, allspice, cloves, and cinnamon on a large skillet over medium heat for 2 minutes or until fragrant. Stir frequently.

3. Add cumin and stir, toasting for 1 minute. Remove spices from heat and transfer to a molcajete or spice grinder. Grind into a powder consistency. Set aside.

4. Toast 1 cup pepitas on a large skillet over medium heat. Stir frequently until fragrant and begin to brown, about 2 minutes. Remove pepitas from skillet into a separate bowl.

5. Repeat with 4 tablespoons sesame seeds, stirring frequently, toasting for 1 minute or until golden brown. Transfer sesame seeds to bowl with pepitas. Set aside.

6. Repeat with 1/3 cup peanuts, stirring frequently, toasting for 2 minutes. Transfer peanuts to bowl with pepitas and sesame seeds.

7. Over medium heat, heat 1/4 cup oil in the same skillet used to toast seeds and peanuts. Add garlic and fry for 1 minute.

8. Add onion and stir. Fry for 2 minutes more or until onion begins to soften. Remove onions and garlic into a separate container and set aside.

9. Using the same skillet and oil, fry the slices of bolillo over medium heat until golden, about 2 minutes on each side. Remove and set aside.

10. Reduce heat to low. Continuing to use the same skillet and oil, lightly fry the dried morita and chipotle chiles until both hydrate and swell.

11. Add the ancho chiles and quickly fry on both sides, about 2 minutes. Do not burn.

12. Add 1 cup water and cover to finish hydrating. Simmer for 5 minutes. Turn heat off and let them cool for 10 minutes.

13. Add tomatoes, spices, seeds, peanuts, garlic, onion, bread slices, hydrated chiles, and broth to a blender. Blend until smooth. If your blender container is too small to fit all ingredients, blend in batches.

14. Strain blended sauce through a mesh strainer into a large bowl.

15. Heat 1/4 cup oil in a large saucepan over medium heat. Carefully pour sauce into saucepan and stir. Season with salt or bouillon. Continuously stir for 15 minutes to mix well and avoid sticking to saucepan. (If you'd like to add meat, you can add precooked chicken or turkey to the sauce at this point and simmer over medium-low heat for another 10 minutes.)

16. Garnish with a sprinkle of remaining pepitas, sesame seeds, and peanuts.

Mole Manchamanteles

TABLECLOTH STAINER

Due to its deep red color, this mole is called manchamanteles, *which means "tablecloth stainer." The mixture of flavors from ancho chiles, roasted tomatoes, spices, nuts, raisins, and sweet fruit is a divine, complex sauce that can be poured over cooked chicken, turkey, or pork.* Manchamanteles *is different from a traditional mole because it includes sweet fruit during the cooking process. It is typically reserved for special occasions and celebrations.*

—*Ericka*

8 Roma tomatoes, stem scars removed

4 cups water

8 dried ancho chiles, wiped clean; stems, veins, and seeds removed

1/2 cup + 2 tablespoons vegetable oil, divided

1 medium white onion, cut in large slices

6 cloves of garlic

1/4 cup raw almonds, blanched

1/4 cup raw peanuts, shelled

1/4 cup raisins

1 day-old bolillo, sliced

4 whole cloves

8 whole allspice

10 peppercorns

1/4 teaspoon dried oregano

1 cinnamon stick

3 cups chicken broth, divided

1 1/2 teaspoons sea salt

3 tablespoons sugar

2 tablespoons apple cider vinegar

1 large ripe plantain, peeled and sliced in 1-inch pieces

2 cups chopped pineapple

1 small green apple, peeled, diced

1 small pear, peeled, diced

Prep time: 30 minutes
Cook time: 1 hour, 30 minutes
Yields: 6 cups
Spice level: 🌙

1. Roast tomatoes on a comal over medium heat. Turn with tongs until char spots form. Remove from heat and set aside.

2. Bring water to a boil in a medium saucepan. Turn heat off as soon as the water boils.

3. Place ancho chile skins on hot comal, 2–3 at a time, for 30 seconds on each side until skins soften. Do not burn. Transfer to saucepan with hot water and let hydrate for 30 minutes.

4. Heat 2 tablespoons oil in a large skillet over medium heat. Add onion and garlic. Cook until tender, about 5 minutes. Do not burn. Remove using a slotted spoon and transfer to large bowl. Set aside.

5. Reduce skillet heat to medium-low. Add almonds and peanuts; lightly fry for 2 minutes. Remove using a slotted spoon and transfer to a separate bowl.

6. Add raisins to skillet and lightly fry for 1 minute. When raisins begin to puff up, remove from skillet using a slotted spoon and transfer to the bowl with almonds and peanuts.

7. In the same skillet over medium heat, lightly fry the bolillo slices until golden brown. Transfer to the bowl containing the nuts and raisins.

8. Place cloves, allspice, peppercorns, oregano, and cinnamon in a spice grinder or a molcajete. Process into a fine powder.

9. Place tomatoes, onion, garlic, nuts, raisins, and 1 cup chicken broth in a blender. Blend until smooth and then run through a strainer into a large bowl. Set aside.

10. Add hydrated chiles, bolillo slices, spices, and 2 cups chicken broth to a blender. Blend until smooth and then run through a strainer into the bowl with tomato mixture. Stir to mix well.

11. Heat 1/4 cup oil in a large saucepan over medium-low heat. Add sauce, salt, sugar, and apple cider vinegar. Stir to mix well. Simmer for 30 minutes.

12. Heat remaining 1/4 cup oil in a large skillet. Add plantains and fry until golden brown. Remove plantains and transfer to a paper towel–lined plate to drain excess oil.

13. Add pineapple to sauce and cook for 10 minutes.

14. Add plantain, apple, and pear slices to sauce. Cook for 5 minutes or until sauce begins to simmer.

15. Serve over cooked chicken, turkey, or pork.

Mole Poblano
PUEBLA–STYLE MOLE

Mole poblano is one of the most delicious sauces I've ever tasted! It's smoky, spicy, rich, and sweet—perfect for a special occasion. I make a big batch of this silky smooth sauce and freeze for whenever a craving arises. This sauce can be served over turkey, chicken, pork, beef, and even vegetables, such as roasted potatoes, cooked mushrooms, or sautéed squash. Don't forget a side of rice and a sprinkle of sesame seeds; it's delightful!
—*Ericka*

Prep time: 30 minutes
Cook time: 1 hour, 15 minutes
Yields: 8 cups
Spice level: 🌶

1/3 cup sesame seeds
6 cups water
1 tablet (90 grams) Mexican chocolate
3 ounces piloncillo cone
3/4 cup + 1 tablespoon vegetable oil, divided
5 mulato chiles, stems, veins, and seeds removed
5 pasilla chiles, stems, veins, and seeds removed
4 ancho chiles, stems, veins, and seeds removed
2 dried chipotle chiles, stems, veins, and seeds removed
3 dried árbol chiles, stems removed
1/3 cup raw peanuts, shelled
1/3 cup raw almonds, shelled
1/3 cup raisins
1 day-old corn tortilla
1 small day-old bolillo, sliced

20 Mexican animal cookies
1/3 cup sliced white onion
3 cloves of garlic
1 ripe plantain, peeled and sliced
6 whole cloves
6 peppercorns
2 whole allspice
1/4 teaspoon coriander seeds
1/8 teaspoon anise seeds
1 teaspoon dried oregano
1/4 teaspoon ground cinnamon
8 cups chicken broth
1 tablespoon sea salt
1 tablespoon chicken bouillon

1. Heat a skillet over medium heat. Add sesame seeds and toast, stirring frequently until lightly golden, about 2 minutes. Transfer to a large bowl and set aside.

2. Bring water to a boil in a large saucepan. Turn heat off.

3. Remove 1 cup hot water into a medium bowl. Add chocolate tablet and piloncillo to dissolve. Set aside.

4. Add 1/4 cup oil to skillet over medium heat. Fry the mulato, pasilla, ancho, and chipotle chile skins for about 8 seconds on each side and the árbol chiles for 6 seconds on each side, turning frequently. Do not burn. Transfer chiles to the saucepan with hot water to hydrate for 30 minutes.

5. Add 2 tablespoons oil to skillet over medium heat. Fry peanuts, almonds, and raisins for 1 minute, stirring frequently. Using a slotted spoon, transfer into the saucepan where chiles are hydrating.

6. Heat 2 tablespoons oil in skillet over medium heat. Fry the tortilla and bolillo slices for 20 seconds each. Transfer to saucepan where chiles are hydrating.

7. Decrease heat to medium-low and fry animal cookies for 15 seconds, stirring frequently. Using a slotted spoon, transfer to saucepan where chiles are hydrating.

8. Add 2 tablespoons oil to skillet, increase heat to medium, and add onion and garlic. Fry until lightly golden. Using a slotted spoon, transfer to saucepan where chiles are hydrating.

9. Fry plantain slices for 15 seconds on each side. Transfer to saucepan where chiles are hydrating.

10. Decrease skillet heat to medium-low. Add cloves, peppercorns, allspice, coriander, and anise and fry for 10 seconds, stirring frequently. Transfer to saucepan where chiles are hydrating.

11. Add oregano and cinnamon to saucepan where chiles are hydrating.

12. Heat 3 tablespoons oil in a separate large saucepan over low heat.

13. While the oil is heating, add the contents of the large saucepan, toasted sesame seeds, dissolved chocolate and piloncillo, and broth to a blender and blend until completely smooth. Transfer blended mixture into the saucepan with oil. Season with salt and bouillon.

14. Increase the heat to medium and cook sauce, stirring frequently. Adjust salt if necessary.

15. Simmer for 25 minutes, continuing to stir. Keep warm. Serve over your favorite protein with a sprinkle of sesame seeds and a side of rice.

Mole de Cacahuate
PEANUT MOLE

Delicious peanut mole is a hearty, nutty sauce with just a small touch of spice. It is absolutely delicious and can be poured over chicken, turkey, or roasted vegetables.

—Nicole

Prep time: *10 minutes*
Cook time: *1 hour*
Rest time: *5 minutes*
Yields: *6 1/2 cups*
Spice level: 🌶

2 1/2 tablespoons oil, divided
1 medium onion, quartered
3 cloves of garlic
3 whole allspice
1/2 Mexican cinnamon stick, broken in pieces
2 cups unsalted peanuts, shelled

3 small Roma tomatoes
7 small-medium dried guajillo chiles, stems and seeds removed
2 árbol chiles, stems removed
4 cups broth, divided
3/4 teaspoon salt

1. In a large frying pan over medium heat, add 1/2 tablespoon oil and fry the onion, garlic, allspice, and cinnamon until lightly toasted and fragrant, about 2 minutes.

2. Add the peanuts and cook for 4 minutes. Transfer mixture to blender.

3. In a large frying pan over medium heat, fry the tomatoes in 1 tablespoon oil until they soften and brown, about 10 minutes, turning occasionally.

4. Add guajillo and árbol chiles and allow to cook with tomatoes for about 2 minutes before pouring in 3 cups broth. Bring to a boil; then lower heat to low and simmer for 20 minutes.

5. Transfer tomato-chile mixture to blender with peanut mixture. Blend on high until smooth.

6. Once a uniform mixture is obtained, add remaining 1 cup broth and salt. Blend again for 1 minute to combine.

7. Place saucepan over low heat and add 1 tablespoon oil. Pour peanut mole into saucepan and fry for about 15 minutes, stirring often.

8. Remove from heat and allow to rest for 5 minutes before serving.

Make It Spicy

Jalapeños Confitados
CANDIED JALAPEÑOS

My mouth waters at just the thought of candied jalapeños. I could eat this sweet-spicy condiment straight out of the jar, but they taste ideal in a sandwich or burger. You be the judge. You can make a batch ahead of time and keep them in the refrigerator or share a jar with a friend.
—Nicole

Prep time: 10 minutes
Cook time: 20 minutes
Yields: 3 1/2 cups
Spice level: 🌙

2 pounds jalapeño chiles
2 cups apple cider vinegar
2 cups granulated sugar
1 cup dark brown sugar

2 teaspoons salt
1/2 teaspoon coriander seeds
2 cloves of garlic, slightly smashed

1. Rinse jalapeños under cold water to remove any debris. Dry with a paper towel.

2. Remove stem from each jalapeño; then cut into 1/4-inch round coins.

3. In a dutch oven over a medium-high heat, mix apple cider vinegar, sugar, brown sugar, salt, and coriander. Mix until all sugar dissolves, about 5 minutes, and allow mixture to come to a boil.

4. Add jalapeño slices and allow mixture to come back to a boil. Cook for 10–15 minutes or until the jalapeños have shrunken a little bit.

5. Using a slotted spoon, remove all the jalapeño slices and divide them equally between two 16-ounce jars. Add 1 clove of garlic to each jar.

6. Continue boiling liquid for about 8 minutes to allow syrup to thicken.

7. Pour syrup over jalapeños and garlic; then push the jalapeños down to make sure all the jalapeños are covered in syrup.

8. Bring to room temperature and then seal. It can be stored in the refrigerator for up to a month.

Queso de Habanero

HABANERO-SPICED CHEESE

For many years I would buy a spicy cheese spread from the market, but I wasn't always fortunate enough to come across it in the aisles. So one day, I decided to make my own. This is the best recipe to serve to a group of guests. Watch it disappear in minutes!
—Nicole

Prep time: 30 minutes
Chill time: Overnight
Yields: 2 cups
Spice level:

4 ounces cream cheese, room temperature
5 ounces goat cheese, room temperature
1 1/2 cups shredded gouda cheese
3 tablespoons minced green onion
1 habanero pepper, stem, seeds, and ribs removed; minced

1/8 teaspoon garlic powder
1/8 teaspoon salt
1/4 teaspoon black pepper
1/4 cup dried cranberries

1. In a medium mixing bowl, mix together cream cheese and goat cheese.

2. Fold in gouda cheese and mix to combine.

3. Add in remaining ingredients and mix until fully combined.

4. Place in refrigerator overnight to chill.

5. Serve with crackers.

Miel Picosa
HOT HONEY

Miel picosa is one of my favorite spicy-sweet condiments. I use it in a variety of ways: drizzled over milanesa, *in a fresh batch of carnitas, or on* elotes *off the grill. It tastes excellent swirled into a cup of ginger tea or as the base of a homemade salad dressing. You can even pour a little over your freshly popped popcorn!*

—Nicole

Prep time: *10 minutes*
Cook time: *5 minutes*
Cool time: *1 hour*
Yields: *1 cup*
Spice level: 🌙

6 pequín chiles
1 árbol chile

1 cup honey

1. Heat a comal over medium heat. Add chiles and toast for 5 minutes or until fragrant.

2. Grind the chiles using a molcajete.

3. Pour honey and chiles into a small pot over medium heat.

4. Simmer for 5 minutes, allowing the chile to perfume the honey. Do not let the honey boil.

5. Remove from heat and allow to come to room temperature, at least 1 hour.

   Tip: *Miel picosa* can be stored in a cool, dry place in an airtight glass jar.

Chocolate Azteca

SPICY MEXICAN HOT CHOCOLATE

This Spicy Mexican Hot Chocolate is the perfect way to warm up during the cold months. It takes regular chocolate caliente *and gives a welcomed spicy kick to each sip.*

—*Nicole*

Prep time: 5 minutes
Cook time: 20 minutes
Yields: 5 cups
Spice level: 🌶

I cup water
2 árbol chiles, broken in half
4 tablets (3.1 ounces each) Mexican chocolate tablets

4 cups milk
1/2 teaspoon ground chile powder, divided

1. Pour water and árbol chiles into a medium pot over medium-high heat and bring to a boil. Once boiling, lower the heat to simmer.

2. Add in Mexican chocolate tablets and stir until chocolate melts completely.

3. Pour in milk and continue stirring, allowing mixture to get hot.

4. Remove mixture from heat and strain into a pitcher to discard chile pieces and seeds.

5. Use a *molinillo*, or whisk, to create a froth in the chocolate.

6. Pour into 4 mugs and dust the top of each cup with 1/8 teaspoon ground chile powder.

Acknowledgments

My Deepest Gratitude . . .

Thank you to my forever partner, Mando; I love our life together and feel so grateful I get to spend it with you. You are an amazing dad to our son and show me your love in your daily actions. Thanks for photographing all my recipes for this book—you're the best!

Thank you, Max, for being such a loving teenager whose smile lights up every room. You make motherhood my treasured gift, and I can't imagine my universe without you in it. I can't wait to see where this life takes you, and I'll be here cheering you on all the way. I love you so much, my precious boy.

Thank you, Mom, for raising me in your quick wit and boundless creativity. You taught me the true meaning of unconditional love and loyalty. Thank you for teaching me the importance of self-worth and strength. I love you so much, Mom, and I will be by your side for as long as I'm alive.

Thank you to my *tios*, *tias*, and Nina Diana for helping raise me . . . it really does take a village, and I think you all did a good job. Hee-hee!

Thank you to my brother and sisters for divulging in our twisted humor with me for all these years. Chicano Presleys . . . I love you!

Thank you to all my *primos hermanos* who cared for me and put up with my nonstop talking and singing when we were kids. You babies truly make my heart explode!

Thank you to the Lopez, Caldera, and Flores families for loving me and allowing me to love you all back. I'm honored to be a part of this beautiful family.

To my *comadres*, Maria and Liz . . . I love you both to the ends of this earth and cherish our special bond.

Thank you to my GIRL FRIENDS for being the best *hermana*-hood a girl could ask for. You all continue to expand my universe with your intelligent perspectives, abundance of kindness, and sensitive hearts (superpower)! A-dre, Angie V., Denise F., Gabriela V., Gicel M., Lou C., Lucy G., Mari C., Marie M., Monica R., Monique F., Nancy A., Natalia C., Rachel M., Sylvia G., and Tonantzin R. . . . Where would I be without you all?

Thank you to Familius: Christopher Robbins, Ashley Mireles-Guerrero, Brooke Jorden, and Peg Sandkam! I am grateful for the opportunity to publish this cookbook with Familius.

Love,

Nicole

Thank you, Mamá Amelia, for your precious molcajete. It was my source of inspiration to learn how to make all types of salsas with it. I continue to use it and continue to learn from it. I will cherish it always. I hope you are proud. *Te extraño*.

Mami. *Estoy tan agradecida contigo*. Thank you for your continued guidance in the kitchen and support in all aspects of my life. You are my pillar of strength, my best friend, and an inspiration as one of the hardest-working women I know. You amaze me with your resilience, and I aspire to be just like you. *¡Te amo!*

To the love of my life, Efrain. Thank you for all the support in this crazy journey we have together. You are a wonderful husband and an exemplary father. Joaquín has the best dad and I the best husband. *¡Te amo!*

Joaquín. *¡Mi Kikín!* Thank you for being the best, most helpful, and dedicated son. Thank you for all your assistance with this book. You did a lot of spice grinding and cleanup as I tested recipes. I love you! Continue being the way you are, and you will go far in life. Don't lose sight of your creativity and passion for sculpting, playing the piano and ukulele, and boxing!

To my sister, Telma, thank you for your words of encouragement and your support. I look forward to our chats and crazy antics.

To my brother-in-law, Aaron, the guy who eats the hottest salsas, thank you for all your support and encouraging me to add more chile to my salsas. *¡Que pique!*

To my sweet Sophie and spicy Frida. Love you! Continue being curious and keep asking questions. Remember to continue being creative. Love you to the moon and back! Let's go, Hot Dogs!

Dave Sanchez and Dave Zavala. I know I always have your support. Thank you for the fun and laughter. It means a lot to me, and I look forward to your visits.

Celeste Musick, my friend I can always count on. Thank you so much for your help, support, and taste-testing for my books. I am so lucky to have found a friend like you. Our friendship means the world to me.

Thank you, Lilly Ayala, for your friendship and continued support. Your delightful attitude is a bright light in my life and always keeps me positive.

Thank you to my friend, executive producer, and director Lisa-Renee Ramirez for breaking me out of my shell and trusting me with your vision. Never in a million years did I ever think I would be doing what I'm doing today, and I have you to thank for it. *¡Chiquita pero picosa!*

Keda. My MVP! Thank you so much for all your help. I could not have done it without you. I love your passion for cooking and your calming demeanor that keeps me happy during those frenzied cooking moments.

Thank you, Neda, for all your help and positive affirmations. You always know how to keep the positivity going. Thank you so much for appreciating my food! I will cook for you anytime!

Thank you, Gordon, Bud, and Shane—the best film crew! Thank you for all your hard work and dedication. You guys are unbelievably talented and so much fun to work with.

Thank you to the brands that continue to place their trust in me and support me in my passion. Jennifer Giambroni, you were the first. I appreciate and value our partnership all these years. You say "Queso!," I say "Count me in!"

Kimberley O'Quinn. Thank you for the continued partnership. You keep my workflow sweet! I look forward to working with you time and time again.

¡Gracias Roble Mantecon! Por todo tu apoyo y confianza todos esto años.

To Llyr Heller-Humphreys at the Los Angeles Public Library. Who knew that our friendship would lead to us working together?! Thank you so much for letting me spread the word about the beauty of Mexican cooking. I really appreciate all you've done for me and my books.

To the Familius family: Christopher Robbins, Ashley Mireles-Guerrero, Peg Sandkam, and Brooke Jorden. Thank you for opening your arms wide open and welcoming me into your family. I appreciate all you've done for me and my passion for cooking.

Ericka

About the Authors

Ericka Sanchez is a recipe developer, food stylist, food photographer, host of the award-winning television show 'Ericka's Mexican Cocina' and creator of Nibbles and Feasts. Ericka was born in Torreon Coahuila, Mexico, and immigrated with her family to El Paso, Texas, at eight years old.

Ericka's website revolves around her life as a bicultural Latina living in California and began as a way to catalog recipes and cherished memories in the kitchen with her grandmother, Amelia, and mother, Carmen, in Mexico. Now her recipe development has led her to reconnect with her Mexican roots by developing her own twist on the traditional.

Ericka has a marketing and social media background, having worked in sports marketing, retail property management, and community management for 20 years.

Her website, recipes, food styling, and photography have led her to work with Fortune 500 companies and a feature in the award-winning Allen Media Group's Recipe. TV network. Her and her work has been featured in various online and print magazines such as *Oprah Daily*, *Parents Latina*, *Taste of Home*, *Eating Well*, *Cosmopolitan for Latinas*, *Woman's Day*, *SHAPE*, and *Latina*. She is a regular contributor to the award-winning recipe websites Yummly, Simply Recipes, and Food 52.

Ericka is the author of three other cookbooks: *Aguas Frescas & Paletas*, *!Buenos Días!* and Golden Poppy Award nominee *¡Buen Provecho!*.

Ericka Lives in Orange County, California with her husband, Efrain; her teenage son, Joaquin; and her two dog rescues, Captain and Chopper.

Born and raised in Los Angeles's eastside, Nicole Presley is a Latina culinary enthusiast and recipe developer passionate about her culture and food. She is self-taught and inspired to keep the traditional Mexican desserts of her childhood alive with her recipes. She is also a master of Mexican-American fusion desserts to honor her dual cultures and take your taste buds on a magnificent culinary journey.

Nicole uses her skills that combine cooking and beautiful food art to create accessible recipes for thousands of followers on her social media platforms, known as Presley's Pantry. She has been hired by some of the country's most renowned companies as a food stylist and recipe developer, and has landed her some of the most incredible experiences that continue to shape her footprint in the culinary world. In her first book, *¡Viva Desserts!*, Nicole used her personal and professional experiences to create decadent desserts from her East LA kitchen that pay homage to her roots and celebrate all the sweetness life has to offer.

Nicole lives in East Los Angeles with her husband, her teenage son, and her two chihuahuas.

VISIT OUR WEBSITE WWW.FAMILIUS.COM

Familius is a global trade publishing company that publishes books and other content to help families be happy. We believe that happy families are key to a better society and the foundation of a happy life. The greatest work anyone will ever do will be within the walls of his or her own home. And we don't mean vacuuming! We recognize that every family looks different and passionately believe in helping all families find greater joy, whatever their situation. To that end, we publish beautiful books that help families live our 10 Habits of Happy Family Life: *love together, play together, learn together, work together, talk together, heal together, read together, eat together, give together,* and *laugh together.* Further, Familius does not discriminate on the basis of race, color, religion, gender, age, nationality, disability, caste, or sexual orientation in any of its activities or operations. Founded in 2012, Familius is located in Sanger, California.

CONNECT

Facebook: www.facebook.com/familiusbooks
Pinterest: www.pinterest.com/familiusbooks
Instagram: @FamiliusBooks
TikTok: @FamiliusBooks

The most important work you ever do will be within the walls of your own home.